THE SEW HELPFUL SERIES

BLOUSES, SHIRTS & TOPS

Simple Sewing & Serging Techniques

by Laurie Pat McWilliams

Sterling Publishing Co. Inc., New York

A Sterling/Sewing Information Resources Book

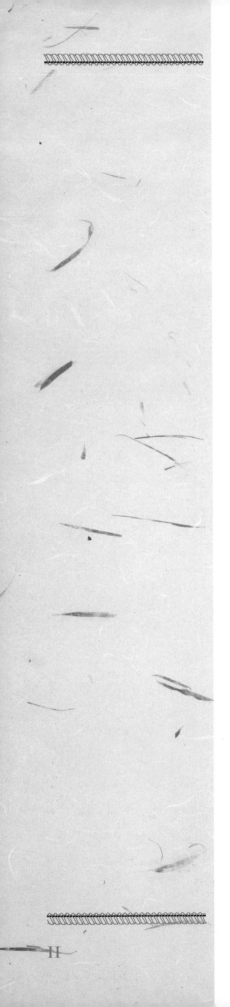

Sewing Information Resources

Editor: JoAnn Pugh-Gannon
Photography: Kaz Ayukawa, K Graphics
Cover Photography: Chris Shorten Photography
Production provided by Jennings and Keefe
Publishing Director: Jack Jennings
Project Manager: Janet Andrews
Cover and Text Design: Jim Love/Studio Arno
Electronic Composition: Studio Arno

Library of Congress Cataloging-in-Publication Data Available
2 4 6 8 10 9 7 5 3 1

A Sterling/Sewing Information Resources Book

Published by Sterling Publishing Company, Inc.
387 Park Avenue, New York, NY 10016
Produced by Sewing Information Resources
P.O. Box 330, Wasco, Il. 60183
Distributed in Canada by Sterling Publishing
c/o Canadian Manda Group, One Atlantic Avenue, Suite 105
Toronto, Ontario, Canada, M6K 3E7
Distributed in Great Britain and Europe by Cassell PLC
Wellington House, 125 Strand, London, WC2R 0BB, England
Distributed in Australia by Capricorn Link (Australia) Pty Ltd.
P.O. Box 6651, Baulkham Hills, Business Centre, NSW 2153, Australia
Printed in Hong Kong.

Sterling ISBN: 0-8069-6168-6

DEDICATION

To my Mom, Jennie Simpson,
who wouldn't buy me all the clothes I wanted.

ACKNOWLEDGMENTS

Special thanks to my son, Joel, for coming back home
and enabling me to sleep at night.
To my good friends, Warren and Chris Shutt, for their modeling and
photography skills. Also to my editor, JoAnn Pugh-Gannon, for her faith
in me from day one. All the samples in this book were sewn by the author,
Dorothy Cusic and Bonnie Wink.

PART ONE

Contents

ABOUT THE AUTHOR

Laurie Pat McWilliams learned to sew when she was six years old while living in Taiwan with her parents. With no television or shopping readily available at that time, what was a little girl to do? So Laurie entertained herself by making doll clothes from her old outfits.

After receiving a degree in Clothing and Textiles from Southwest Missouri State University, Laurie began her professional sewing career as a supervisor in a garment factory. She gained additional experience with factory techniques while working as Costume Supervisor at Silver Dollar City in Branson, Missouri. Indulging her passion for fabrics, Laurie was then employed as a buyer at nationally known Baer Fabrics in Lexington, Kentucky. From Baer's, Laurie spent the last five years as a Bernina of America Sewing Specialist, traveling the country conducting seminars and product training sessions for both Bernina retailers and consumers. Over the last decade, many enthusiastic home sewers have shared in Laurie's love for sewing.

Laurie has written numerous sewing articles and designed several patterns distributed through Bernina of America. Her first book was titled *Keep It Sew Simple Garment, Construction and Tailoring*. And she contributed to the recently published Rodale book, *Quick Gifts, Make Today—Give Tomorrow*.

PART ONE

Laurie's Approach
to Sewing Fun

Sewing Notions and
Machine Accessories

How to Use
This Book

So Where
Do You Start

Caring for Your
Creations

Sewing
Essentials

Working with
Commercial Patterns

Pressing

Laurie's Approach to Sewing Fun

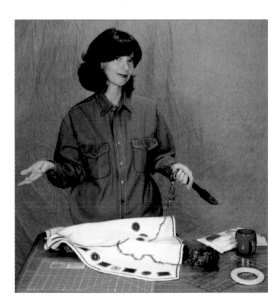

"I don't have time to sew!"

I hear this statement often. But really, consider how much time you spend shopping. You drive to the mall, find a parking spot, find the store you want, choose the styles you like, the color, the size, and the price. Then, you have to take your clothes off to try things on! Next you decide you'd better check other stores too. Before you know it, it's time for lunch. After your lunch break, you finally make your decision. You are now ready to proudly wear your new purchase to *the* party. Guess what? Someone is wearing the same outfit, but two sizes smaller!

My dear mother has the saddest story of all. She went to a Christmas party at the Officer's Club, a special event for which she'd splurged on a new gold lame´ dress. When she got to the party, she discovered that all the waitresses were wearing the same dress! True story. Just ask her, she remembers!

"I don't have the patience to sew."

Another often-heard remark. My first question is usually "What kind of a sewing machine do you own?" "Is it your grandmother's or a find from a garage sale?" If your machine is not your friend, get rid of it. Sell it, donate it–then shop for a new one. Buy a machine that works, one that has well-balanced thread tension. You need a machine that you'll enjoy spending time with, that you're comfortable using, that you can bond with. You may not necessarily need all the gadgets, although they can be fun to use. I find if the feature I want is not built-in, I don't bother to use it. Be sure to investigate used machines, too.

"I *love* to sew!"

Sewing gives me great pleasure. It's my time to be alone and be creative. It's a very personal way for me to express myself. I know my body, I know my style, I know me. Sewing is my therapy. So...enjoy yourself...express yourself. Enjoy SEWING!

"So, what if you make mistakes?"

Don't be afraid to make mistakes. You may be trying new techniques, patterns, or styles, or may be working with a new fabric. Mistakes happen to everyone. But don't let them stop you from sewing again.

- Use the Three-Foot Rule: If you can't see the mistake from three feet away, it's fine!
- Wear it and say you bought it.
- Be creative. Embellish over mismatched plaids or cover tears or holes.
- Remake the garment into a child's outfit or doll clothes.
- Put it in your quilt stash for future use.
- Forget it! But remember to learn from your mistakes.

BLOUSES, SHIRTS & TOPS

How to Use This Book

I suggest you read the following sections first to help ensure your sewing success: "So Where Do You Start?," and "Working With Patterns."

WHAT'S NEXT?

1. First, select your pattern. Carefully read the section about fabrics on the back of the envelope and compare the pattern company's suggestions to the chapter in this book on "Styles of Blouses, Shirts, and Tops."

2. Select and buy your fabric and all of the notions, except buttons.

3. Pretreat the fabric and the notions, see "Caring for Your Creation."

4. Read through the pattern instructions carefully and study the pattern layout.

5. Press the fabric and pattern pieces.

6. Lay out the fabric and pattern and carefully cut out each piece. This is a very important step, since making a mistake with the scissors could be disastrous.

7. Mark dots, center front, pocket placement, darts, and any design lines. Refer to "Working with Patterns." Remember, the dots on the collar pieces are very important.

8. Cut out any interfacing and lining pieces.

9. Fuse the interfacing to all appropriate pieces.

10. Sew the collar ("Collars and Necklines," page 45), pockets ("Pockets," page 51), and add design extras, like piping or ruffles ("Designer Details," page 81).

11. Sew the darts ("Sewing Essentials," page 27), and any front or back design details.

12. Sew on the pockets.

13. Sew the back seam or sew the keyhole neckline opening ("Collars and Necklines," page 47).

14. Sew the shoulder seams.

15. Finish the front facing or front band, then sew on the collar ("Collars and Necklines," page 46).

16. Attach the sleeves if using the flat method ("Sleeves," page 59).

17. Sew the side seams ("Seams," page 55).

18. Set-in the sleeve if using the round method ("Sleeves," page 60).

19. Hem the sleeves or add the cuffs ("Sleeves" or "Hems," pages 63–71).

20. Press, edgestitch, and/or topstitch.

21. Select the buttons. Sew the buttonholes and attach the buttons ("Buttons and Buttonholes," page 77).

Your blouse, shirt, or top is now complete!

Laurie's Tips

I'm often asked which sewing machine to buy. I always recommend the following: Pick a store close to your home that sells sewing machines and has knowledgeable salespeople who you are comfortable talking with. Check out their mechanic. Do they offer classes? Ask to talk to some of their machine customers. What do they think about the store and its service? The extras a friendly, reputable sewing store can offer make all the difference.

When looking at machines, I like a built-in buttonhole, numerous needle positions for attaching zippers and edgestitching, and an alphabet for labeling my garments with the pattern number and date. And, if you like large letters, a built-in monogram capability is nice for pockets and cuffs.

So Where Do You Start?

EQUIPMENT

Buy the best sewing equipment you can afford

- A sewing machine with well-balanced thread tension
- An iron with steam control
- A pair of good, sharp scissors that fit your hand
- Extra packages of sewing machine needles in different sizes and types
- Smooth straight pins

Nice extras

- A 3/4 thread serger (overlock machine) with differential feed
- A cutting table (adjusted to your height)
- A large, self-healing cutting mat and rotary cutter
- A pair of appliqué scissors

SELECTING FABRIC

Always buy the best quality fabric you can afford. On the back of the pattern envelope is a list of recommended fabrics appropriate to that style. These fabrics are suggested so you can achieve the best look and fit possible. You may, however, select similar fabrics that will drape or conform like the recom-

mended fabrics. But remember, when using plaids or stripes extra fabric may be required. If you're not sure of the fabric's quality or suitability for a particular pattern, ask a knowledgeable salesperson at your favorite fabric store.

IDENTIFYING FABRICS

Sometimes it's difficult to identify the fabric content of the beautiful yardage you've just purchased. The content information is important so you know how to take care of your fabric before and after construction.

Laurie's Tips

Owning a serger is like having a microwave oven in your kitchen. First, you think you don't need it; then, you don't know how to use it; and now, you can't live without it because it saves you so much time! I prefer a 3/4 thread model with easy stitch conversion possibilities for rolled hem and flat lock. Simple tension controls are a must along with easy threading. Differential feed makes working with knits or finer fabrics much easier, preventing ripples or gathers. If you are just starting to use a serger, lessons from your dealer can make learning the "ins and outs" of your machine much simpler.

The following basic test helps, however, with blends it is less accurate.

With tweezers, hold a 2″ scrap of your fabric over a candle. Once it ignites, move it over a fireproof container and observe the results. See Table 1.

If you suspect acetate fibers, drop a scrap into nail polish remover. The fibers should disintegrate.

FABRIC PREPARATION

Preshrink your fabric before you begin your sewing project. Wool and suit-weight fabrics should be dry-cleaned; otherwise, washing your fabric according to the fabric care-code on the end of the bolt is sufficient. If the fabric is highly embellished, very ornate, or has other unique characteristics (e.g., vinyls), I often don't pretreat the fabric knowing I won't be washing or dry-cleaning the garment later. But then I am very careful when and where I wear this special piece!

Once preshrunk, fold the fabric right sides together selvage to selvage and store until you're ready to begin cutting.

	TABLE 1	
	Burn Test Results	
Plant Fiber	Cotton Linen, Rayon	Burns quickly with flame Smells like burning paper
Animal Fiber	Wool Silk	Burns slowly without flame Smells like burning hair
Synthetics	Polyester Micro fibers and many others	Fibers melt without flame Leaves a hard bead instead of ash

INTERFACING

Interfacing is used to give support or structure to a garment. It also prevents wrinkling and stretching in the interfaced area. If you're questioning whether to interface or not-interface. The area will hold up longer.

Your first decision when buying interfacing is whether to purchase woven, non-woven, or fusible knit interfacing. Often, this decison is based on your preference and what is available at your local fabric store. Handle the interfacing and fashion fabric together as one. A good guideline for choosing the correct weight of interfacing is to select one that is lighter than the fashion fabric but will drape and wash like the fabric. If you've selected a fusible knit interfacing, it literally becomes a "second skin" and adds a slight weight but great stability to your fabric.

Your second decision is which to buy, fusible or sew-in. If the fabric won't take high heat, it's best to purchase a sew-in. Fusibles are wonderful, but the fashion fabric must be able to take heat, moisture, and pressure.

Self interfacing is another option. A piece of the fashion fabric itself is used for the interfacing. Many designers use this method. This is a particularly good idea if the fabric is sheer or of an unusual color. Also, don't be afraid to use more than one kind or type of interfacing together to achieve the result you want.

Interfacing should be pretreated just like the fashion fabric. If it's a sew-in type, preshrink it like the fabric. If it's a fusible, it also needs to be preshrunk. Place the fusible interfacing in a pan of warm water and soak for 10 minutes. Wring out the excess water and hang to dry. Follow the fusing instructions on page 33.

Laurie's Tips

I prefer iron-on interfacing for most everything. They save time in your sewing but do require fusing. When fusing, do it slowly. Pick up the iron and set it down, don't glide. Follow the manufacturer's instructions. If you make a fusing mistake (fuse where you didn't mean to fuse!), hold the iron above the interfacing, shoot steam down onto the interfacing and then gently pull it away from the fabric.

Blouses: *The more feminine blouse needs interfacing in the collar or at the neckline opening, cuffs or along the sleeve edges.*

Shirts: *The classic shirt should be interfaced in the collar, cuffs, button and buttonhole areas, and possibly the pockets. Choose an interfacing that is lighter weight than the shirt fabric. Use two layers in the collar and cuffs for a crisper look.*

Tops: *If the top you've chosen doesn't have a rib trim, interface the neckline facing pieces if a facing is used.*

Working with Commercial Patterns

CHOOSING THE CORRECT SIZE

It can be difficult to decide which is the correct size pattern for you. As a rule of thumb, choose the pattern which is closest to your bust measurement. If you're between sizes, buy the smaller size. Why? Ease. All the pattern companies add allowances to their patterns for comfort and style which is called ease.

Read the description of the blouse, shirt, or top located on the back of the pattern envelope. It will state how fitted the garment is when finished. Vogue Patterns define their fit and the included ease as follows:

STYLE	EASE
Close-fitted	0-2⅛″
Fitted	3″ –4″
Semi-fitted	4⅛″ –5″
Loose-fitted	5⅛″ –8″

Minimum bust ease for any blouse should be approximately 2″ to 2½″ except when using a knit fabric.

FITTING

The success of your sewing project depends on how well the garment fits once you're

finished sewing. It's important to understand how to fit a garment before you begin cutting your fabric.

Start by pinning the pattern pieces together, including the sleeve but eliminating the facings, making sure to match the seam lines not the cutting lines. What you have created is a tissue shell which is actually half of your garment.

Try this half pattern on over a body suit or a leotard. Pin the center back line at the nape of your neck and again at the center back waist. Now, look in the mirror and

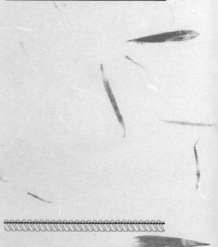

Time-Saver
Buy a cutting table adjusted to your height, a large self-healing cutting mat and rotary cutter.

Adjustment Chart

| LENGTH AND WIDTH | BODY MEASUREMENTS | | ADJUSTMENT |
	YOURS	STANDARD	(+ OR-)
1. **Front length**—from shoulder at base of neck over bust point to waistline			
2. **Shoulder to Bust**—from shoulder at base of neck to bust point			
3. **Back Waist Length**—from prominent bone at back of neck to waist			
4. **Shoulder**—from base of neck to shoulder point			
5. **Back Width**—across back, 5″ (12.5 cm) below base of neck			
6. **Arm Length**—from shoulder point to wrist, over slightly bent elbow			
CIRCUMFERENCE			
7. **Bust**—across fullest part of chest and around back			
8. **Hips**—9″ (23 cm) below waistline, or wherever you are widest			
9. **Upper Arm**—around fullest part			

check the grain line markings indicated on the tissues. Are they straight? If not, re-pin the pattern pieces at the seam lines to make these grain lines hang straight.

By reviewing how the tissue fits your body in the mirror, you'll know which alterations to make on the pattern. For instance, if the pattern is long you should refer to "Altering the Pattern–Length" or if it's too tight across the bust, refer to "Altering the Pattern–Bust Circumference."

Before unpinning the pattern from your leotard to make the adjustments needed, check these other points:

- the sleeve length ending at your wrist-bone when your arm is bent;
- the fit across the bodice, leaving room for shoulder pads;
- the position of the pockets;
- and the fullness across the upper back for movement.

Mark on the pattern tissue the true bust point. Unpin the pattern pieces and lay them flat to make any necessary changes by referring to the section on "Altering the Pattern."

ALTERING THE PATTERN

When altering your pattern tissues, use masking tape, pink hair tape, or special pattern tape available at your local fabric store.

Once you have made all of your adjustments, make sure the pattern pieces still lie flat. If they don't, check your adjustments again and make the necessary corrections.

Don't forget, if one pattern piece is changed be sure to check the adjoining piece(s) for any necessary adjustments.

Length

Lengthen and shorten lines show you where to adjust. Don't forget to adjust all the necessary pattern pieces. For example, if you change the length of the Front, be sure to make the same changes on the Back and the Front Interfacing pieces.

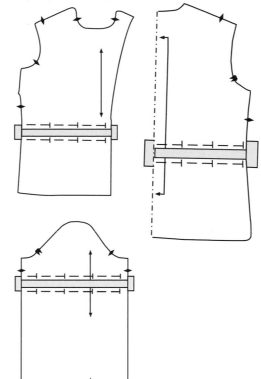

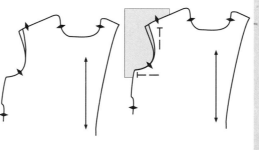

To Lengthen: Cut the pattern apart on the lengthen/shorten line and spread it evenly the needed amount. Pin it to paper and connect the cutting lines.

Width/Shoulder

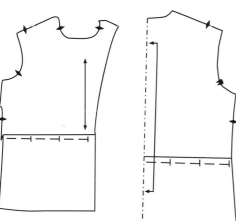

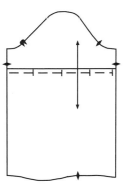

To Shorten: Measure up from the lengthen /shorten line the amount needed and draw a line across the pattern. Fold the pattern on the printed line and bring the fold to the drawn line; pin in place. Redraw cutting lines.

Shorten   Lengthen

Adjust the Front and Back pattern pieces. For adjustments up to ¼", mark the amount needed to shorten or lengthen the shoulder cutting lines at the armhole edge. Draw a new cutting line from the mark, tapering to the original one at the armhole as shown. To adjust more than ¼", see "Shoulders—Broad/Narrow," page 15.

Width/Back

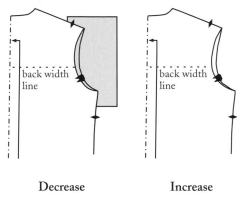

Decrease   Increase

Since you bought the pattern based on your bust measurement, you shouldn't need to make much of a back width adjustment. For changes up to ½″, adjust the Back as follows: To decrease or increase at the back width line, mark half the amount needed in or out from the armhole cutting line. Draw a new cutting line from the mark, tapering back to the original one at the shoulder and the underarm.

Bust Circumference

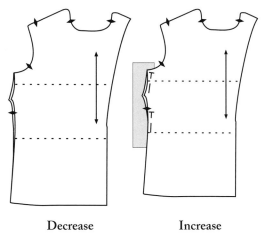

Decrease   Increase

Note: If your bust cup is larger than a C, make the "Large Bust Cup" adjustment instead of this adjustment.

Adjust the bust circumference at the bustline on the Front and Back. To decrease, mark one quarter the amount needed **inside** the side cutting line; to increase, mark one quarter the amount needed **outside** the line.

Correct the cutting lines, tapering back to the original ones at the armhole and waistline.

High or Low Bust

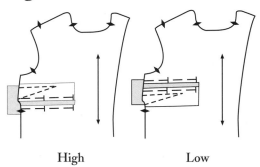

High   Low

If your shoulder to bust measurement is different from the standard (see Adjustment Chart), adjust the darts on the Front pattern. Cut the pattern along the dart box lines. Slide the box up or down the needed amount. Place paper under the pattern and pin cut edges in place. Correct the side seam cutting line.

Large Bust Cup

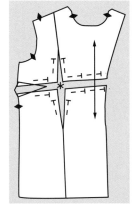

If your bust cup is larger than a C, you may want to adjust the pattern to fit your cup size. First, check your Shoulder to Bust measurement on the Adjustment Chart. If it differs from the standard, adjust the dart (see "High or Low Bust") and draw a new bustline and bustpoint on the Front pattern, higher or lower as needed. Since cup size affects your Front Waist Length and Bust Circumference, you may need to adjust them both. Check the Adjustment column of the chart for the amount to adjust.

On the Front, draw a vertical line from the midpoint of the shoulder to the lower edge. Cut the pattern apart on this line and along the bustline. Adjust Front Waist Length by spreading the pattern along bust-line slash; pin to paper. Then adjust the Bust Circumference half the amount needed by spreading the vertical slash, tapering to nothing at shoulder and lower seam lines. Pin in place. The Front is now longer than the Back. To restore the original side seam length, redraw dart, taking in the amount added. Taper the dart toward the bustpoint, as shown.

Sleeve Circumference

You can only adjust the sleeve up to $\frac{1}{2}''$. Draw a line from the dot at the sleeve cap to the wrist, parallel to the grain line. Cut the pattern on this line.

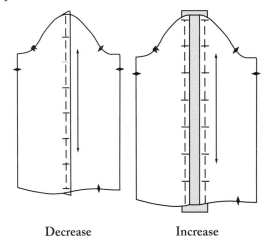

Decrease   Increase

To decrease the sleeve, lap the cut edges the needed amount; to increase, spread them. Pin the edges in place and correct the cap and lower cutting lines.

On the Front and Back patterns, adjust the armhole so the sleeve will fit into it. To decrease, mark half the amount changed on the sleeve inside the side cutting line at the armhole edge. Redraw the cutting lines, tapering to the original ones. Move armhole notches up the same amount you decreased the armhole.

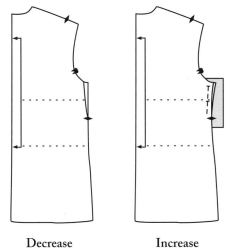

Decrease   Increase

To increase, mark half the amount changed on the sleeve outside the side cutting line at the armhole edge. Redraw the cutting lines, tapering to the original ones. Move armhole notches down the same amount you increased the armhole.

Shoulders–Broad/Narrow

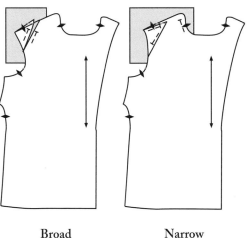

Broad   Narrow

You will only have to make these special adjustments for pronounced figure variations.

If you need to adjust the shoulders more than $\frac{1}{4}''$, adjust the Front and Back patterns as follows:

Draw a diagonal line from the midpoint of the shoulder cutting line to the midpoint of the armhole cutting line as shown; cut the pattern apart on this line. Spread the cut edges (for broad shoulders) or lap them (for narrow shoulders) the needed amount, tapering to nothing at the armhole seam line. Pin in place and correct the shoulder cutting line as shown.

Shoulders–Sloping/Square

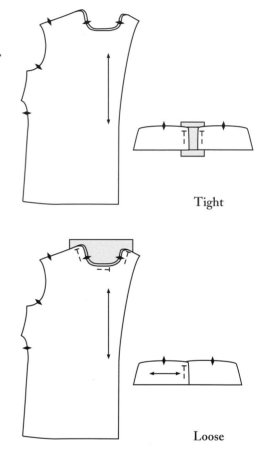

Sloping   Square

To see if your shoulder slope differs from the pattern, pin the Front and Back patterns together at the shoulder and side seams. Clip into the armhole seam allowances and try the pattern on. Ask a friend to pin-mark a new shoulder seam line at a slant that fits you better; this will mark the adjustment you should make. Draw new shoulder cutting lines on the Front and Back patterns as follows: Begin ⅝" above the pin marking at the shoulder end and taper to the original line at the neck edge. This changes the armhole measurement, so you must now restore it to its original size. If you have sloping shoulders, lower the underarm cutting line by the amount you lowered the cutting line at the shoulder end. For square shoulders, raise the underarm cutting line by the amount you raised the cutting line at the shoulder end. Redraw the armhole cutting line, tapering to the original one as shown.

Neckline–Tight/Loose

To see if the pattern neckline fits, pin the Front and Back patterns together at the shoulders. Clip into the neckline seam allowance and try the pattern on. Ask a friend to pin-mark a new seam line. Lower the

Tight

Loose

neckline if it's too tight or raise it if it's too loose. Draw a new cutting line ⅝" above the new seam line. Trace the adjustment on the neck edge of the front extension. To see how much to adjust the collar, measure both the old and new neck seam lines (omitting shoulder seam allowances) on Front and Back; subtract to find the difference. Adjust the collar this amount by cutting the pattern apart along the center back line. Spread the cut edges (for tight neckline) or lap them (for loose neckline). Pin edges in place and correct the cutting lines. Draw a new center back line.

Back—Round/Erect

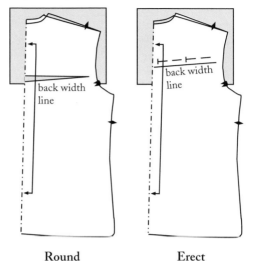

Round   Erect

Pin the Front and Back patterns together at shoulder and side seams. Clip neck and armhole seam allowances. Then, try it on to see how much length to add (for round back) or subtract (for erect back) across the upper part of the Back pattern piece. Have a friend slash and spread the pattern as described below or pinch out the excess. Cut the pattern apart on the back width line. For round back, spread the cut edges at center back and pin in place; for erect back, lap the cut edges. Correct the center back line. Next, restore the original neckline size. Lower (for round back) or raise (for erect back) the shoulder cutting line at the neck edge the amount you changed the neck at center back, tapering the line to the original one at the end of the shoulder.

MARKING

Marking your fabric with all the notches and dots is a very important part of construction. Fold the fabric, right sides together, so you can make your marks on the wrong side. If it's difficult to tell the right from the wrong side, you make the decision. Place a piece of masking tape on the wrong side of the fabric to help you keep all pieces correct side up.

As a time saver, don't cut around the notches on the pattern pieces but nip a $\frac{1}{4}$" clip in the middle of each notch. Be sure to notice that the front of the sleeves and the armholes have a single notch and the back of the sleeves and armholes have a double notch. Clip twice at double notches to prevent setting in your sleeve incorrectly.

There are many types of washable and vanishing marking pens to mark dots and squares on the fabric. Place these marks on the wrong side whenever possible. When marking on white fabrics, always test the fabric and marking tool first.

To mark the center front, any fold lines, pleats or tucks, simply press them into the fabric with your iron.

"Altering the Pattern" information and drawings provided courtesy of Simplicity Pattern Company.
© Copyright 1990–Simplicity Pattern Co., Inc.

Time-Saver

Become familiar with your sewing machine. Take operating lessons from your dealer or read the instruction manual thoroughly. This will eliminate hours of frustration.

Sewing Notions and Machine Accessories

Using the correct needles, threads, and the appropriate presser feet makes your sewing project that much simpler.

NEEDLES

Skipped stitches are often a sign of a problem needle. It's best to start with a new needle before each project and then change the needle frequently. Match the size of the needle to the fabric and thread you've chosen. Then determine the right size needle for the thread; the thread should lie in the long groove on the front of the needle and slide through the eye easily.

Needles are numbered in sizes 60 to 120 and the lower the number the smaller the needle. Larger needles are used for heavier fabrics and smaller needles for finer fabrics. When selecting needles, the first number listed on the package refers to the American system and the second number to the European system (e.g., 11/80).

Needle types refer to the shape of the point. New needle types will be introduced with the development of new fabrics or threads. There are many varieties of needles on the market today.

TABLE 3
Needle Sizes

FABRIC		9/70	11/80	14/90	16/100	18/110
Lightweight	Batiste	✖				
Medium	Challis		✖			
Heavy	Denim			✖		
Very Heavy	Canvas				✖	
Extremely Heavy	Sail cloth					✖

	T A B L E 4			
	Needle Points			
FABRIC	REGULAR	UNIVERSAL	BALL POINT	LEATHER
Woven	✖	✖		
Knit		✖	✖	
Denim	✖	✖		
Leather				✖
Plastic/Vinyl	✖			✖
Sheer	✖			

Following are some commonly used needles:

- Topstitch needles have a larger eye making it easier for the heavier decorative-topstitch threads to pass through smoothly.
- Machine embroidery needles have a larger, rounded eye to keep the metallic threads from breaking.
- Microtex needles are used for sewing on micro-fibers.
- Twin needles are two needles mounted on one shank; they are used for topstitching and pintucks. The size to be used is based on the size of the needles and the distance between the needles (e.g., 2.0/80–2.0 is distance and 80 is needle size).
- Jeans needles are used for sewing tightly woven fabrics.
- Wing needles are flat and wedge-shaped. They push the threads apart making a decorative hole.
- Double wing needles—one needle is a wing needle, the other is a straight needle for decorative stitching.
- Stretch needles have ballpoint tips for sewing knit fabrics.

THREADS

Just as you've chosen quality fabric for your garment, you should also work with quality thread. Good quality thread should be smooth with no thick or thin spots, and should not create much lint. Cotton-wrapped polyester or 100% polyester are good quality threads for general machine stitching. But there are many other types of threads that can be used for special purposes:

- Silk thread has a nice sheen and is strong but can be more expensive.
- Topstitching or buttonhole twist thread is thicker for showing off decorative topstitching.
- Invisible or nylon thread is useful because it's transparent. Be careful not to touch this thread with a hot iron as it will melt.

- Fusible thread is handy and saves time when quick basting with long stitches. Don't use for permanent stitching.
- Textured nylon thread is a soft, stretchy thread that works well in the looper of sergers. It's great for rolled edges.
- Decorative threads come in many sizes referring to the thickness of the thread. Like needles, a numbering system is used to identify the size, but on thread the lower the number, the thicker the thread. Size #40 and #50 are good sizes for general decorative sewing.
- Rayon threads are used for their shine and are available in great colors. They come in size #30 or #40.
- Metallic thread is used for sparkle.

Laurie's Tips

When sewing with metallic threads, be sure to use a topstitching or embroidery needle and loosen the top tension of the machine.

Time-Saver

Try to use fewer straight pins, using weights when possible.

SEWING MACHINE FEET

Here is a short list of helpful, extra feet that will make your sewing easier and faster.

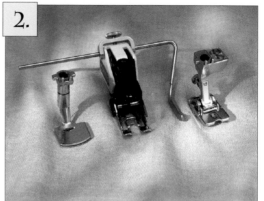

1. **Edgestitch** or **topstitch** foot includes a bar for straight, even guiding while stitching.

2. **Gathering**, **piping**, and **walking** feet are used to gather lengths of fabric, create piping easily because of the design of the foot, and keep all layers of fabric together without slippage, respectively.

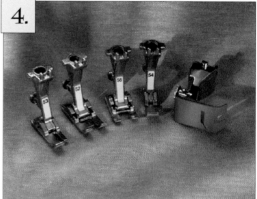

3. **Clear** or **open embroidery** feet provide better visibility when sewing decorative stitches; the **button sew-on** foot creates a thread shank when sewing on buttons by machine.

4. **Teflon-coated** feet won't stick to plastic or vinyls while sewing because the soles are Teflon-coated. Very helpful when sewing on suedes.

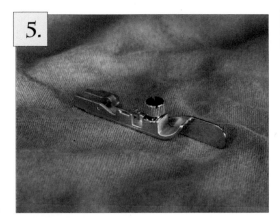

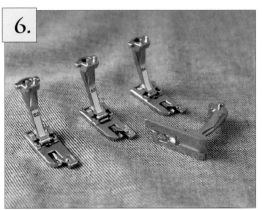

5. **Serger blind hem** foot's adjustable blade guides the fold of the fabric so the needle will just stitch into the edge and stitching will not be seen.

6. **Hemmer** feet double turn the fabric and sew a narrow hem at the same time. The appropriate foot is chosen by the weight of the fabric and the size of the groove on the bottom of the foot.

USING A SERGER WITH COMMERCIAL PATTERNS

If you are the proud owner of a serger or overlock machine, the first question asked is: "How do I use it along with my regular sewing patterns and know how much to trim off?"

Most sergers today have markings on the front of the machine, within easy view, indicating seam allowance increments. These marks are measured from the point of the needle insertion. The presser foot is usually marked showing the position of the needles, both right and left. All of these marks help you in guiding your fabric for serging and trimming along the typical ⅝" seam line, or whatever seam allowance you've chosen.

> **Time-Saver**
> *Buy a serger with a differential feed feature and learn how to use it properly.*

Sewing
Essentials

BIAS STRIPS

Bias strips can be cut any width based on the finished piping size you need. They are used for ruffles, facings, and piping.

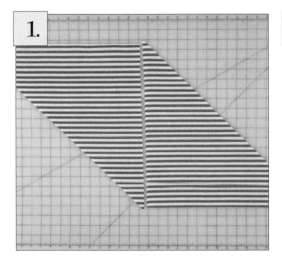

1. Cut a square of fabric and press in half diagonally matching edges. Cut on this press line. Sew straight edges, right sides together, with a ¼″ seam creating a parallelogram.

2. Determine the width you need for the bias strips, and draw lines parallel to the long raw edges. Cut with a rotary cutter and a ruler. Sew strips end to end to make the length you need.

CLIPPING CURVES

Begin by sewing the curved seam using directional stitching. Press the stitches flat as sewn.

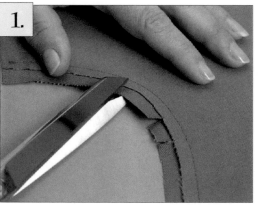

1. **Inward curves:** Clip into the seam allowance at intervals and grade the seams. Press the seam open.

2. **Outward curves:** Cut small wedges of the fabric from the seam allowance creating a smooth curve when turned. Press.

DIRECTIONAL SEWING

Directional sewing should be used for topstitching, edge stitching, and sewing seams.

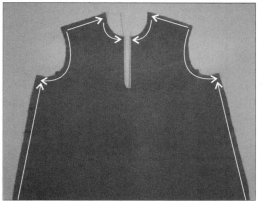

When stitching seams, stitch in the direction of the grain of the fabric. When edgestitching or topstitching, always stitch in the same direction on both sides of a garment.

EDGESTITCHING

Edgestitching is a line of stitches sewn very close to the edge on the right side of the garment; often used on cuffs or collars.

Select your edgestitch foot and position the needle $\frac{1}{16}''$ to $\frac{1}{8}''$ from the garment edge. Always use directional sewing when edgestitching.

DARTS

Darts can add fullness and shape to a garment.

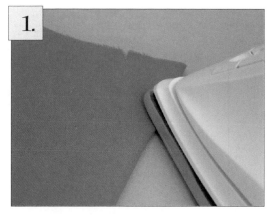

1. Mark a dot with chalk at the point of the dart and clip notches along the fabric edge. Match the notches, right sides together, and press in the dart.

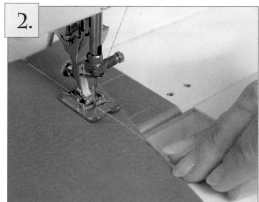

2. Beginning at the notches sew one stitch. Pull the top thread tail until the bobbin thread comes up through the fabric. Pull the bobbin thread to the chalk dot at the point of the dart. Holding the thread taut, stitch using this thread as a guide. Finish stitching off the fabric. Tie off the thread ends.

GRADING SEAM ALLOWANCES

Use this technique on collars and cuffs.

Trim each seam allowance at a different

width to eliminate bulk. To trim the seam allowances in one step, hold your scissors at a 45° angle to the seam; cut both edges together.

SEWING CORNERS

Collars and cuffs demand sharp, pointed corners.

As you get close to the corner, shorten

the stitch length while you are stitching. Take one or two diagonal stitches at the corner. Trim the fabric diagonally at the corner before turning.

Time Saver

Invest in the sewing machine presser feet that you'll need most often. They'll save you time and help make the sewing process easier in the long run.

STAYSTITCHING

Staystitching is a row of straight stitches sewn within the seam allowance which keeps the edge of the piece from stretching

out of shape during construction, as in a neckline.

When clipping a curve very close to the seam line, staystitch next to the seam line to keep the fabric from raveling.

STITCH-IN-THE-DITCH

Use the stitch-in-the-ditch method to secure facings and keep elastic flat in casings.

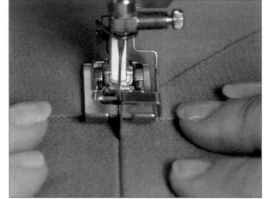

Stitch from the right side of the garment so the needle pierces the well of the seam. The stitches should disappear in the ditch.

TOPSTITCHING

Topstitching is a line of stitches visible on the right side of a garment adding a sporty design detail.

Using an edgestitch foot for your machine,

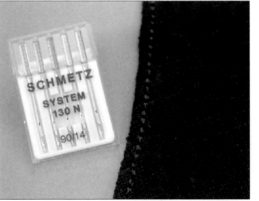

adjust the straight edge on the foot to guide the fabric for an even stitch line. Select a longer stitch length of about 3 mm. Move the needle position, usually ¼″ from the edge. Sew using directional sewing.

UNDERSTITCHING

Understitching is a line of straight stitches sewn from the right side on the facing holding it in place and keeping it from rolling to the outside.

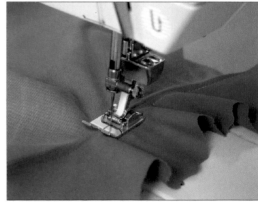

The facing and the seam allowance are pressed away from the garment. A row of stitches is then sewn very close to the seam, on the facing side, through the seam allowance.

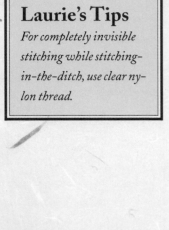

Laurie's Tips

For completely invisible stitching while stitching-in-the-ditch, use clear nylon thread.

Laurie's Tips

Try heavier topstitching thread in the needle and on the bobbin in areas where both sides of the collar or cuffs may show.

SEAM FINISHES

There are basically three ways to finish the raw edges of a regular seam, pinking, serging or zigzaging. Be sure to finish each seam before crossing it with another seam, such as at the underarm and sleeve.

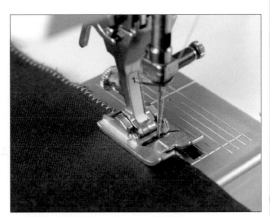

Pinking: After the seam is sewn, using pinking shears, trim the two seam allowances together. Press open.

Zigzaging: If you want to serge or zigzag the seam allowance it is easier to do this before any seams are sewn. Zigzag around each pattern piece then assemble the blouse. Don't stitch around the armhole, the sleeve cap, the neckline, or the collar.

Serging: When serging use only three threads and the left needle. Trim some fabric while serging but remember to then adjust the size of your seam allowance. For example, if you trim $\frac{1}{4}''$ while finishing the edges, you will then sew a $\frac{1}{2}''$ seam instead of a $\frac{5}{8}''$ one.

Pressing

Pressing as you go will prevent your garment from looking "homemade."

EQUIPMENT

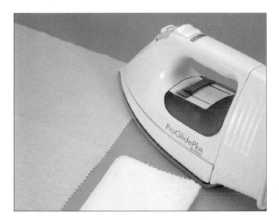

Iron: There are a number of important features to consider before purchasing an iron for your sewing, such as a shot of steam, good weight, and a nice point for pressing in small areas.

Pressing ham: A pressing ham is used for shaping fabric into curves. Seams that need a gentle curve, sleeve caps that are slightly rounded, or darts are best pressed on a pressing ham.

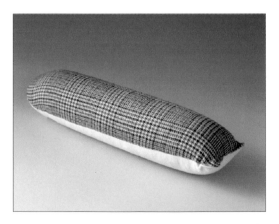

Seam roll: A seam roll is used for pressing seams open and preventing the edges of the seam allowance from being pressed down.

Press cloth: A press cloth is used for pressing delicate fabrics.

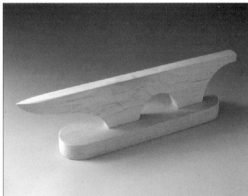

Wooden clapper: A wooden clapper is used to flatten thick areas and keep creases in by trapping steam into the fabric.

PRESSING STRAIGHT SEAMS

Press most seams open before you turn the fabric or cross that seam with another.

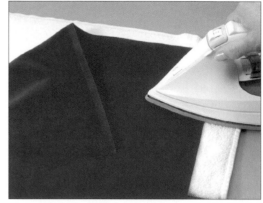

Press the seam open from the wrong side on top of a seam roll, using the tip of the iron and going with the grain of the fabric. Press the seam only, not the edges. Let the seam allowance fall away eliminating edge impressions on the right side of the garment.

When pressing fabrics with nap, such as corduroy or velvet, lay a thick bath towel on the ironing board to prevent the nap from being flattened and dulled.

PRESSING ROUNDED SEAMS

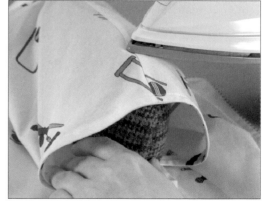

If the fabric is very delicate, place a strip of adding machine tape under the seam allowance to prevent impressions.

Press curved seams, or darts that will be covering a rounded area, over a pressing ham. Press and shape the area right from the start.

FUSING

There must be moisture, pressure, and heat for success when fusing.

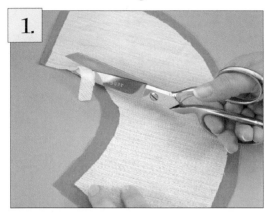

1. When applying fusible interfacing, trim most of the seam allowance away from the interfacing (e.g., cut ½″ from the ⅝″ seam allowance).

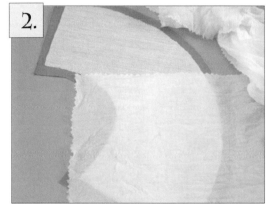

2. Using the steam setting, heat the iron to the highest setting the fabric will allow. If the fabric can't handle a hot iron, use a damp press cloth.

3. Start fusing from the center and work to the outer edges. Pick up the iron and put it down. Do not drag or push the iron. Press down in each area for about ten seconds.

PRESSING DARTS

Press vertical darts, tucks, and pleats toward the center.

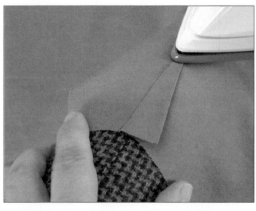

Press horizontal darts, tucks, and pleats down toward the hemline.

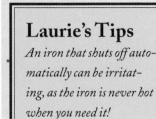

Laurie's Tips

An iron that shuts off auto-matically can be irritat-ing, as the iron is never hot when you need it!

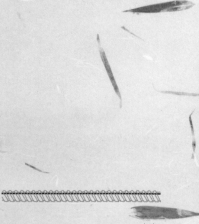

Laurie's Tips

If you've fused something incorrectly, try this: Hold the iron above the inter-facing and shoot it with steam. Carefully peel the interfacing loose while it's still warm. It should pull away easily.

QUILT SOAP

ORVUS paste contains no phosphorus ... ... cate fabrics. The surfactants in ORVUS ...
... gradable.

... shake bottle several times before each use. Highly concen...
... Quilt Soap with the water. Gently place quilt ...
... gentle cycle for 6 to 7 minutes only. ... 1 Tablespoon of Quilt Soap, only.
... if quilt is heavily soiled, wash twice. Do not ...
... antique quilts should be handled gently and ...
... with water using 1 Tablespoon of Quilt Soa...
... fill the layered quilt. Gently hand press down ...
... thru water. Rinse the quilt several ...
... Press squeeze out excess water. Dra...
... water thru water. Do not ...
... OUT OF REACH OF CHILDREN. AVO...
... Y WITH WATER. HARMFUL...
Made in U.S.A. Contents: Sodium L...
... Inc. 2322 N.E. 22nd AV...

Janie
DRY STICK
SPOT
CLEANER

SAFE FOR ALL FABRICS
... NEVER EVER LEAVES A...
... REMOVES MOST GR...
... GRIMY DIRT AND E...
Net...

Caring for Your Creations

FABRICS

The simplest way to become familiar with fabrics is by touching and observing. Notice how the fabric reacts after repeated washings or dry cleanings. Notice what fabric feels good on your body when you're wearing a garment. Remember what fabrics looked or draped the best on your body. I definitely have my favorites! And you will too.

Fibers make up fabrics. Basically fibers can be divided into two groups: natural and manufactured. Natural fibers are either from plant or animal sources. Manufactured fibers are made from chemicals. Today, fabrics are becoming much more complex than ever before. Scientists are working constantly to combine fibers into new blends incorporating the best aspects of both groups.

Table 5 lists some of the characteristics of fibers that will help you when choosing fabrics for your next project.

TABLE 5
Fabric/Fiber Characteristics

NATURAL FIBERS FROM ANIMALS	NATURAL FIBERS FROM PLANTS	MAN-MADE FIBERS FROM NATURAL SOURCES	MANUFACTURED FIBERS
Silk	Cotton	Rayon	Polyester
Wool	Linen	Viscose	Nylon
Hair Fibers	Jute	Cuprarammonium	Acrylic
Camel	Ramie	Acetate	Modacrylic
Mohair		Triacetate	Spandex
Cashmere		Glass	Olefin
		Metal	Rubber
			Teflon

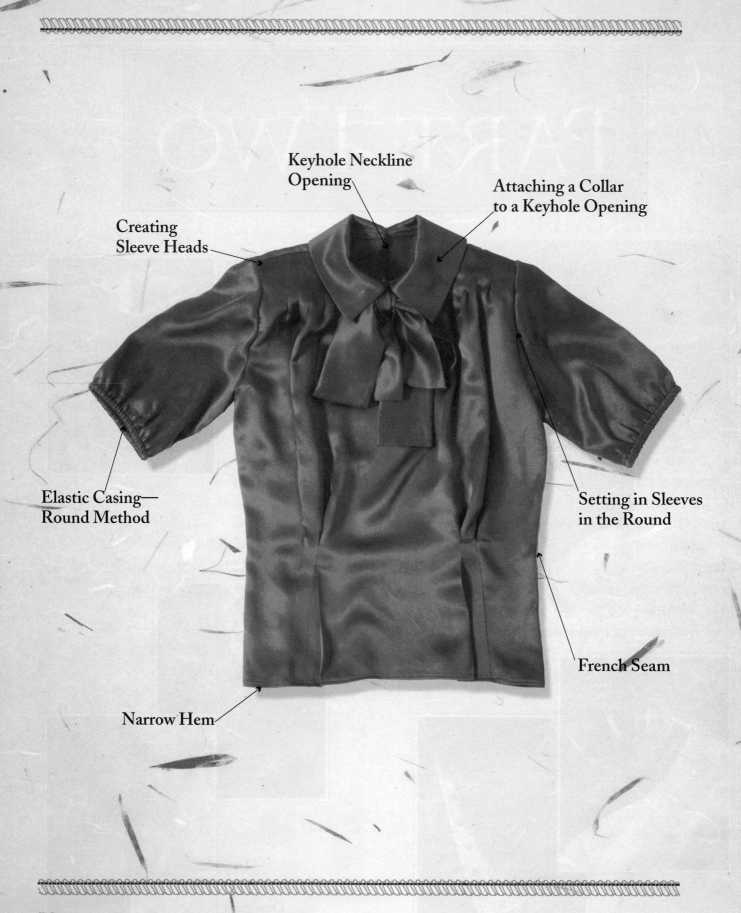

Keyhole Neckline
Opening

Attaching a Collar
to a Keyhole Opening

Creating
Sleeve Heads

Elastic Casing—
Round Method

Setting in Sleeves
in the Round

French Seam

Narrow Hem

The Blouse

Soft, feminine, a variety of collar styles,
optional design details

FABRIC SELECTION

Gauze: casual, sporty
Interfacing choice: woven

Micro fibers: drapes well, luxurious
Interfacing choice: tricot knit

Chiffon: dressy, elegant
Interfacing choice: self fabric

Challis: soft, flowing
Interfacing choice: woven

Techniques

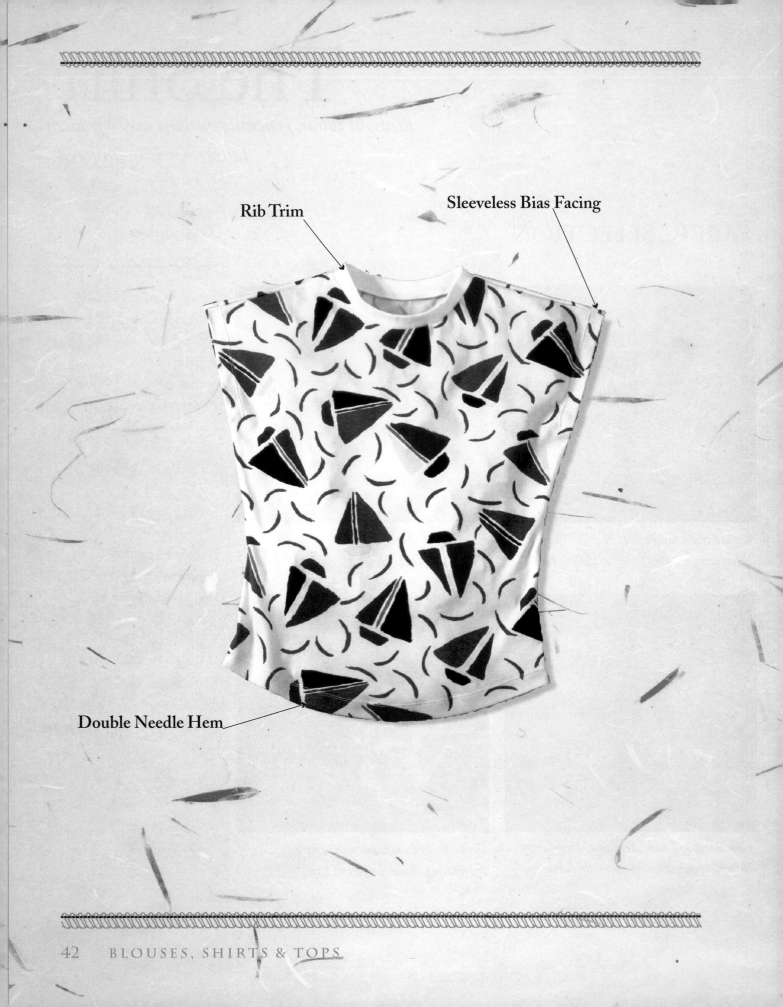

Rib Trim

Sleeveless Bias Facing

Double Needle Hem

The Top

Simple, sleeveless, slips over the head or buttons down the back, usually without collar

FABRIC SELECTION

Charmeuse: shiny, dressy
Interfacing choice: woven

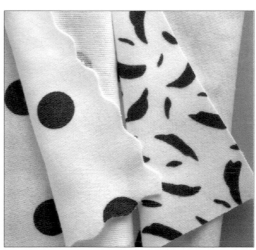

Single knits: stretchy, sporty
Interfacing choice: tricot knit

Jersey: soft, drapes well
Interfacing choice: tricot knit

Double knit: firm, heavier than single knits,
both sides look the same
Interfacing choice: tricot knit

Techniques

Collars and Necklines

STRAIGHT COLLAR

This is the most frequently sewn collar style used on shirts. When using this method, the undercollar won't be visible from the top.

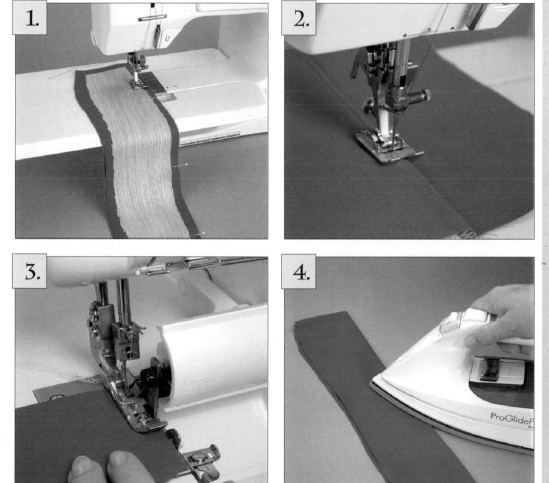

1. Working with any shirt pattern, interface the undercollar only. Sew or serge the undercollar to the uppercollar, right sides together, on the outer edge only.

2. Press the seam allowance toward the under collar. Topstitch from the right side of the undercollar catching the seam allowance in the stitching.

3. With right sides together, sew or serge both ends of the collar.

4. Turn the collar piece to the right side and press flat.

ATTACHING A COLLAR TO A SHIRT FRONT

After completing the collar using the Straight Collar technique, attach the collar piece to a shirt for a tailored look.

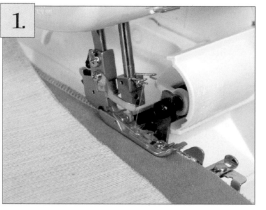

1. Interface the shirt front facing pieces. Clean finish the raw edges of the facing pieces with the serger. Sew the shoulder seams.

2. Pin the finished collar to the shirt neckline. Fold the front facings back over the collar at the fold line and pin. Stitch the collar and facing to the neckline at the ⅝″ seam line. Serge the raw edges together next to the stitching line, trimming a small amount.

3. Turn right sides out. Press the collar up and the seam allowance down.

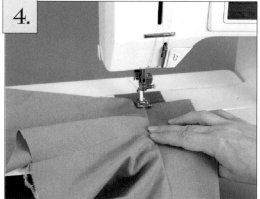

4. Topstitch the seam allowance to the garment from the right side under the collar.

KEYHOLE NECKLINE OPENING

This simple neckline finish is appropriate for a shell blouse. It can be applied to the front or back of the blouse and used in combination with a collar, if desired, or simple bias trim.

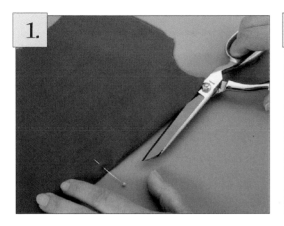

1. Slice along the keyhole line as marked on the pattern piece.

2. Serge using the rolled hem setting along the keyhole opening slash, leaving a long, serger chained tail at one end.

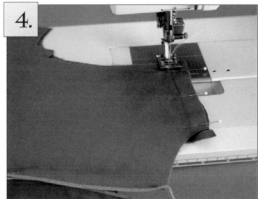

3. Stitch a dart approximately 3″ in length starting 1″ above the bottom of the keyhole opening.

4. After sewing shoulder seams, finish the neckline edge using Sleeveless Bias Facing technique on page 61 or Attaching a Collar to a Keyhole Opening, page 48.

Pockets

LINED PATCH POCKETS

When sewing patch pockets, it can be tricky to get the rounded edges smooth or keep the corners flat. In most instances, it's actually easier to line the whole pocket.

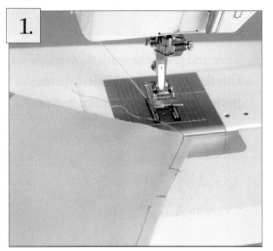

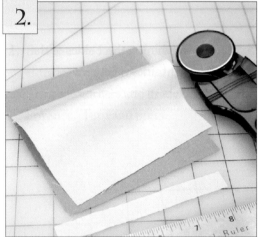

1. Cut a lining piece from the pocket pattern eliminating the top facing. Cut the pocket piece from the fashion fabric. Stitch the lining to the top edge of the pocket piece, right sides together, using a ¼″ seam allowance and leaving a 2″ opening in the center of the seam.

2. Press the top facing of the pocket down along the fold line, wrong sides together. Trim the bottom edge of the pocket lining to match the pocket.

Seams

FRENCH SEAM

A traditional French seam adds an elegant touch to any garment. It's the ideal seam for transparent fabrics since the seam allowance doesn't show through to the outside.

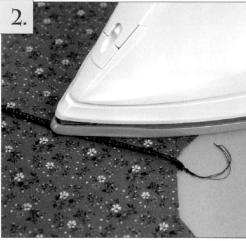

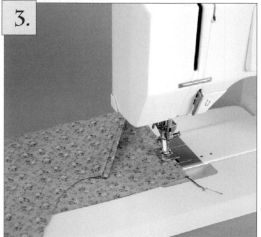

1. Using a three-thread balanced stitch, serge the side seams, wrong sides together, creating a ⅜" seam and trimming off the excess fabric.

2. Press the seams to one side. Press the right sides of the fabric together around the serged seams.

3. With right sides together, use the sewing machine to stitch a ¼" seam encasing the previous stitching.

Laurie's Tips
French seams are perfect for loosely woven or easily-raveled fabrics as the raw edges are completely encased. This seam is suggested for lightweight fabrics only.

MOCK FLAT-FELL SEAM

A flat-fell seam is very durable and gives a garment a sporty look.

Time-Saver

A mock flat-fell seam is the type of seam often used on tailored blouses and shirts. This simple adaptation of that popular seam creates the same look in fewer steps.

1. Set the serger for a three-thread balanced stitch. Serge the side seams, right sides together at the ⅝″ seamline, trimming off any excess seam allowance. Press the seam to one side

2. Topstitch through all three layers of fabric (garment and seam allowance) from the right side of the garment. Stitch one or two parallel rows.

SERGER COVER STITCH SEAM

This unique flat joining seam, created on a serger with a cover stitch, is suitable for knit fabrics and works well in shaped areas such as raglan sleeves or rounded sections, as well as on straight seams.

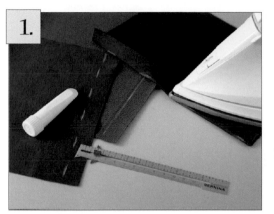

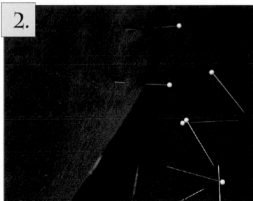

1. Mark the seam allowances at the desired width. Press under the upper fabric at this mark.

2. Place the turned back seam allowance of the upper fabric over the right side of the under fabric, matching the edges.

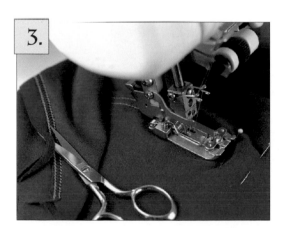

3. Guide the fabric along the edge of the foot for a flat seam. If the seam allowance is more than $\frac{1}{4}''$, trim close to the stitching on the wrong side.

SETTING IN SLEEVES– FLAT METHOD BY SERGER

Ideal for blouse styles requiring gentle ease in the sleeve caps, the sleeves are sewn in flat before the side seams of the garment are sewn.

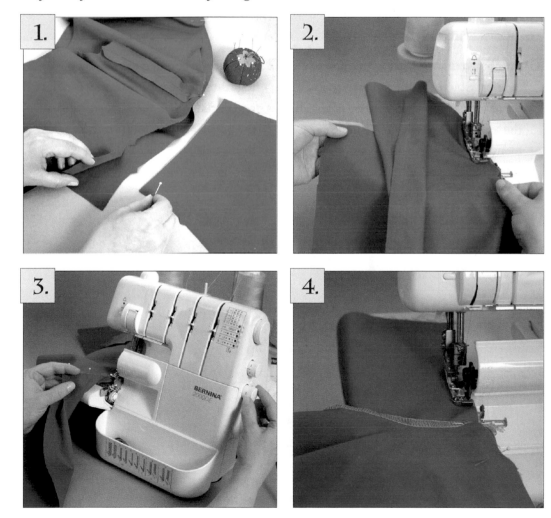

1. Pin the sleeve to the armhole, right sides together, matching all notches and dots.

2. Select a balanced four-thread stitch. Serge the sleeve to the armhole at the $\frac{5}{8}$″ seamline with the sleeve section on top of the feed dogs.

3. Adjust the differential feed to slightly ease the sleeve piece after the first notch. While serging, watch how the piece eases into the armhole. Increase to a higher or lower setting if necessary. Return to the normal setting at the last notch and continue serging to the end of the sleeve.

4. Sew the blouse side seam and the sleeve underarm seam in one complete step.

CREATING SLEEVE HEADS

The purpose of sleeve heads is to keep a very full sleeve cap from drooping.

Laurie's Tips

Sleeve heads should be made from a stiff fabric, like organdy, or a crisp interfacing. If the blouse fabric is sheer, bridal illusion is suggested.

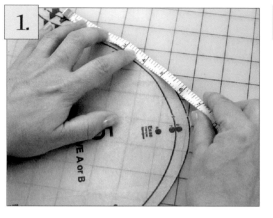

1. Measure the distance from the front notch to the back notch on the sleeve pattern piece.

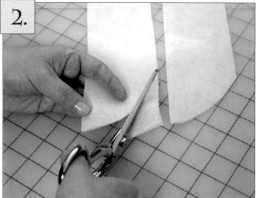

2. Cut a piece of the stiff fabric the measured length by 6″ wide. Fold this rectangular piece in half lengthwise and round off the corners.

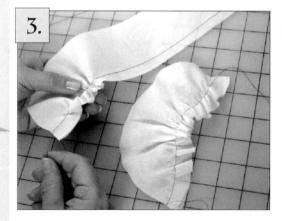

3. Gather the raw edges of the sleeve head together. Attach the gathered sleeves referring to Setting in Sleeves in the Round, page 60. Serge the seam allowances of the armhole and the sleeve together.

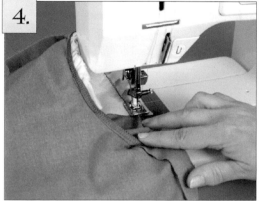

4. Sew the sleeve head to the seam allowance of the sleeve between the notches. Clean finish the raw edges with the serger.

PLACKET

This quick placket application works well on soft, fluid fabrics.

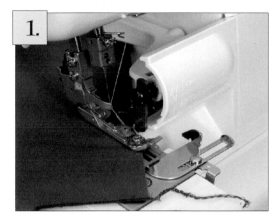

1. Slash the placket opening according to the pattern. Serge the edge of the opening using a narrow three-thread setting on the serger, pulling the slash into a straight line as you serge.

2. Stitch a 1″ long dart starting ¼″ above the bottom of the slash. Press the seam allowance toward the back of the sleeve.

CUFFS

Use the Placket technique along with this cuff application.

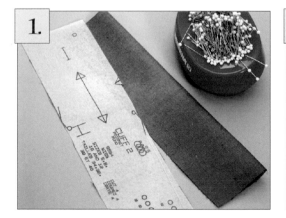

1. Place the seamline of the cuff pattern piece on the fold of your fabric and cut out the cuff.

2. Cut a fusible interfacing for one half of the cuff. Fuse the trimmed interfacing onto the facing half of the cuff, referring to Fusing on page 33.

Time-Saver
Similar to the keyhole neckline opening, the placket can also be finished with the rolled hem on the serger.

Time-Saver
If the pattern you've chosen requires a two-piece cuff, it is much simpler to make a one-piece cuff by eliminating the seam line on the cuff pattern piece.

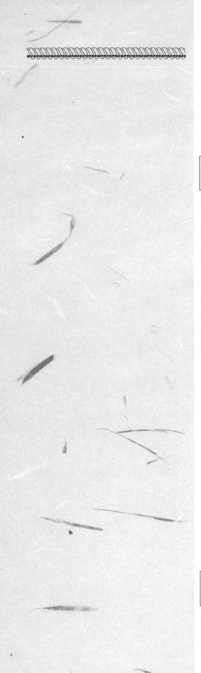

3. Fold the cuff, right sides together, and sew or serge the ends. Trim and grade the seam allowances. Turn and press. Sew the sleeve underarm seam.

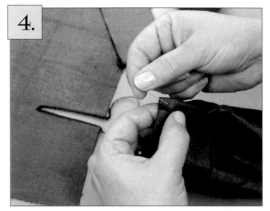

4. Pin the non-interfaced side of the cuff to the sleeve, right sides together. Adjust the gathers or pleats to fit. Wrap the serged edge of the placket around the ends of the cuff.

5. Serge all the layers together using a three- or four-thread balanced stitch.

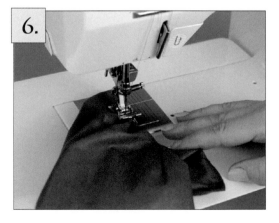

6. Press the seam allowance toward the sleeve. Topstitch the cuff and the placket in one step.

SHOULDER PADS

Adding shoulder pads to a blouse will often help balance your shape. By making the shoulders look wider, the hips will look smaller.

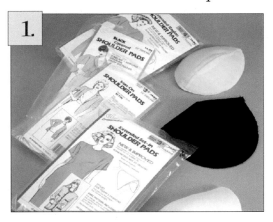

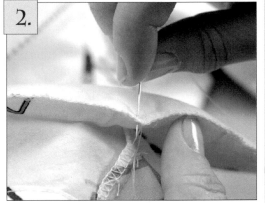

1. Shoulder pads come in many different shapes, such as extended, raglan, kimono, dolman, and set-in styles. Each of these different shapes is available covered or uncovered and in thicknesses from $\frac{1}{4}''$ to $2''$.

2. Try on the blouse and position the shoulder pads to extend about $\frac{1}{8}''$ into the sleeve. Pin the pads in place on the inside of the blouse. Tack the pads to the shoulder seam allowance using loose stitches to allow for a small amount of movement. Tack again to the armhole/sleeve seam allowance in the front and back. Avoid sewing the tacks too tightly creating dimples on the outside of the garment.

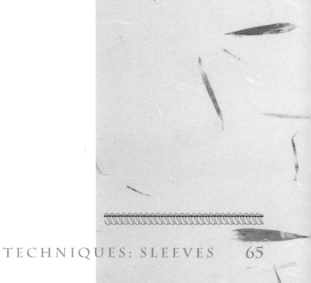

ELASTIC CASING–FLAT METHOD

This method of applying an elastic casing is best for small areas like a cuff, upper arm, or a child's sleeve.

1. Clean finish the bottom edge of the sleeve with the serger. Along the hem line, measure and press up the casing, wrong sides together. Edgestitch ⅛″ from the folded edge.

2. Using a long piece of elastic, mark the wrist or arm measurement adding 1″ for overlap. Do not cut the elastic at this time.

3. Place the end of the measured section of elastic into the casing and stitch across the end to secure.

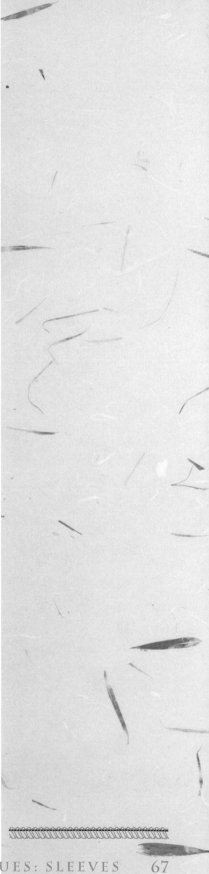

4. Using an edgestitch or zipper foot, stitch while pushing the elastic tightly against the row of edgestitching forming the casing. Be careful not to stitch through the elastic.

5. Pull the elastic through the casing until you see the other measurement mark. Stitch this end of elastic through all thickness ¼″ inside the mark. Cut off the remaining elastic at the mark. Sew the sleeve underarm seam as usual, stitching through all layers.

ELASTIC CASING–ROUND METHOD

This casing technique is very easy to use on the edge of a sleeve or as a waistband treatment at the bottom of a blouse.

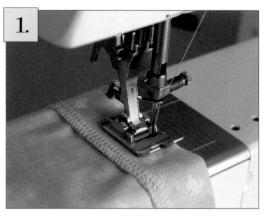

1. Finish the bottom edge of the finished sleeve with the serger. Press up the casing, wrong sides together, along the hem line indicated on the pattern. Edgestitch ⅛″ from the fold.

2. Using a long piece of elastic, mark the wrist or arm circumference adding 1″ for overlap. If this method is being used at the bottom of a blouse, mark the measurement minus 2″. Do not cut the elastic at this time. Place the elastic in the casing against the stitching line. Pin one end of the elastic to the garment.

3. Using an edgestitch or zipper foot, stitch pushing the elastic tightly against the previous stitching line. Be careful not to stitch through the elastic. Stop sewing approximately 2″ from where you started.

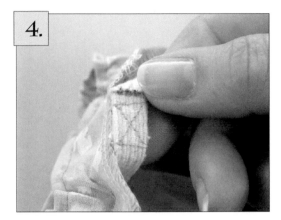

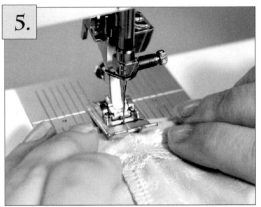

4. Pull the elastic through the casing until you see the mark. Cut the elastic at the mark. Unpin the other end of the elastic and lap both ends approximately ½″ Stitch through the elastic making a square with an X in the center to secure the ends.

5. Finish sewing the last 2″ of the casing. Arrange the gathers evenly and stitch-in-the-ditch at the seam securing the elastic.

Hems

BLIND HEM

When there is a need for a wider hem on a tunic or long over-blouse, or a shirt made from a heavier fabric, this hem technique is frequently used.

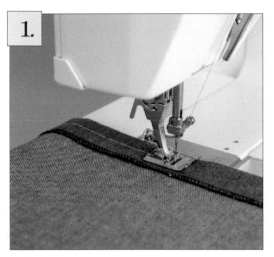

1. Finish the bottom edge of the shirt or blouse with the serger. Measure and press up the hem keeping it approximately 1″ in depth. Baste the hem by machine ½″ from the folded edge.

2. Select your blind hem foot and blind hem stitch. Fold the hem under to the right side of the garment so the serger edge is visible. Place the fabric under the foot with the fold against the guide. The straight stitches should fall on the serged edge and the zig zag should just catch the fold. To adjust the zig zag pick to be invisible, increase or decrease your stitch width.

BLIND HEM BY SERGER

This secure hem is easily sewn in one step and works well on linen or linen-type fabrics.

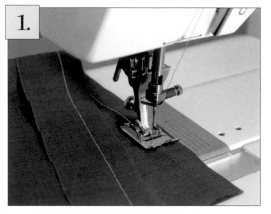

1. Measure and press up the hem keeping it 2″ or less in depth. Baste by machine ½″ from the folded edge. Using your serger blind hem foot, set the machine for flatlock stitching.

2. Fold the hem under to the right side of the garment so only the raw edge is visible. Serge with the needle catching the fold and the blade trimming off the raw edge. Press.

NARROW HEM

Use this technique on lightweight, fluid fabrics.

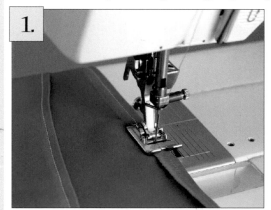

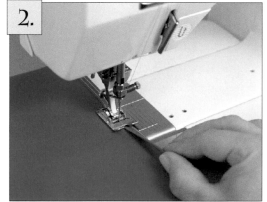

1. Press up ⅜″ along the bottom edge of the blouse or shirt, wrong sides together. Stitch close to the fold. Trim the fabric close to the stitching line.

2. Turn up the hem the width of the first line of stitching and press. Stitch again close to the fold.

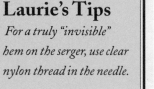

DOUBLE NEEDLE HEM

Suggested primarily for knits, this hem method also works well when sewing on suede and leather.

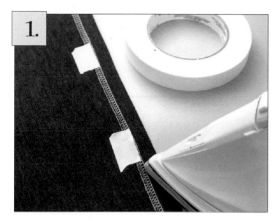

1. Clean finish the raw edge of the hem with the serger. Use the differential feed on the serger for knits or bias-cut fabrics to prevent stretching as you sew. Press the hem up about ⅝″. Tape in place every three inches. Eliminate this step when sewing with suede or leathers.

2. Using a double needle, straight stitch on the right side of the garment along the bottom edge. If a tuck develops between the row of stitches, loosen the top tension or use a double needle with the needles closer together.

ROLLED HEM WITH A HEMMER FOOT

This hem is perfect for linen, lightweight cotton or silk blouses. Hemmer feet are available in a variety of sizes for most brands of sewing machines.

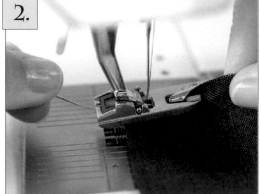

1. Take a few stitches back and forth at the beginning of the hem. Leave about a 3″ length of thread attached to the fabric to help pull it into the "curl" of the hemmer foot.

2. With the hemmer foot on the machine, use the thread tails to pull the fabric into the curl of the foot and past the needle hole. Position the needle to just stitch along the edge of the rolled hem.

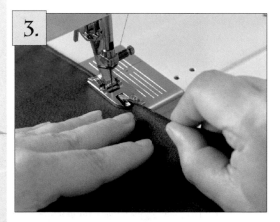

3. Hold the fabric steadily with one hand in front of the foot allowing the fabric to feed smoothly through your fingers.

SERGER ROLLED HEM

A terrific soft edge finish for silky or cotton fabrics.

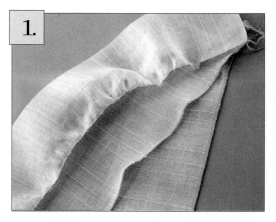

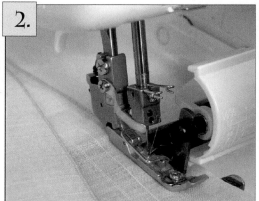

1. Attach the rolled hem foot plate or flip the switch that makes the fabric roll. This adjustment will differ between brands and models of sergers. Set the serger for a three-thread rolled hem. With bias-cut fabric, adjust the differential feed to prevent waves.

2. Serge a rolled edge along the fabric edge trimming off a small amount of the fabric. Always cut off fabric when roll hemming to make a more clean, even hem.

3. To eliminate puckering, loosen the needle tension and shorten the stitch length. Hold the fabric taut.

4. To eliminate "pokeys," which occur more often on the crosswise grain, use a textured nylon thread in the loopers and starch the fabric.

Laurie's Tips

Lightweight knits work well for rolled hems but be careful not to stretch the fabric. Be sure to first test your fabric; if the differential is turned up too much the fabric will gather.

If the fabric won't roll at all, increase the cutting width and use textured nylon thread in the lower looper.

Buttons and Buttonholes

MAKING BUTTONHOLES

*When it comes to choosing between vertical or horizontal buttonholes,
since you are the designer, you get to make that design choice.*

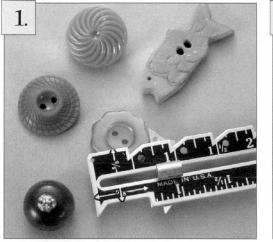

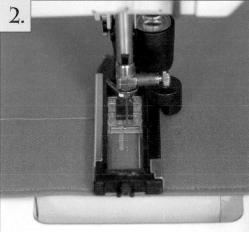

1. Measure the button correctly: *width of button + depth of button = length of buttonhole.* If you don't add the thickness of the button, the buttonhole won't be long enough and will stretch out of shape.

2. When using a sewing machine with a long buttonhole foot, make sure the whole foot is on the fabric sewing towards the edge of the garment. The foot must be totally flat to feed the fabric smoothly.

3. If the fabric has a high nap or uneven weave, place a piece of water-soluble stabilizer between the foot and fabric to even the surface.

ATTACHING FLAT BUTTONS

Flat buttons can easily be sewn on by machine. Most machines have a button sew-on foot and a zig zag stitch or button sew-on program.

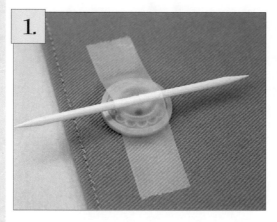

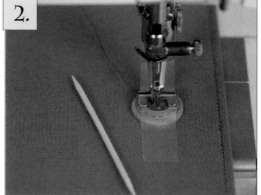

1. To create a shank when sewing on a flat button, place a toothpick between the holes of the button and tape the button in position on the garment.

2. Drop the feed dogs and place the needle in the left hole of the button. Then lower the presser foot. The width of the zigzag will be determined by the space between the holes. Stitch back and forth in each hole four to six times.

3. To tie off, raise the feed dogs and change the setting to a straight stitch, stitch length .01 mm, and needle position, left. Sew three stitches in the same hole. Remove the tape.

ATTACHING SHANK BUTTONS

Unfortunately, shank buttons can't be sewn on by machine!

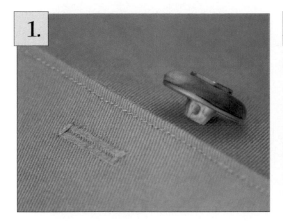

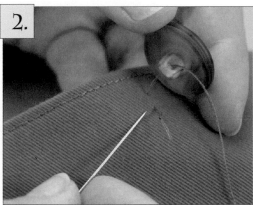

1. The shank of the button lies in the same direction as the buttonhole.

2. Sew the button on with a double strand of thread. Wax the thread for added strength. For high stress areas, dental floss works well as the thread. Start sewing from the right side so the knot will be under the button and won't show from either side.

Laurie's Tips

Horizontal buttonholes should always be used where there will be stress, like on a cuff, at the waist, or on a fitted garment.

Designer Details

HEMMED RUFFLES

This type of ruffle would be used if the fabric is medium to heavy in weight.

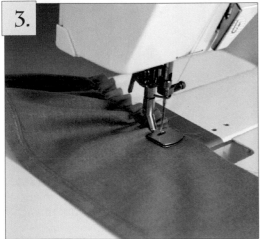

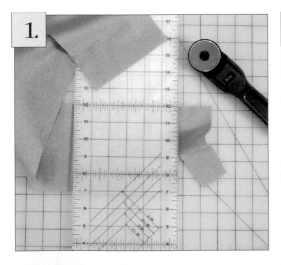

1. Cut a strip of fabric at least twice as long as the finished ruffle. The width should be the finished width plus one seam allowance and hem. If the strip is cut on the bias the ruffles will stand up.

2. Turn under the raw edge along one side of the strip. Turn up the fabric again and stitch in place.

3. Gather the raw edge using the Folded Ruffles method, page 82, or use a gathering foot. With a gathering foot, tighten the top tension and lengthen the stitch. If your machine has a basting stitch, use this for the tightest gathers. Gather the strip and cut off what you need.

FOLDED RUFFLES

This reversible ruffle method is best used on lightweight fabric.

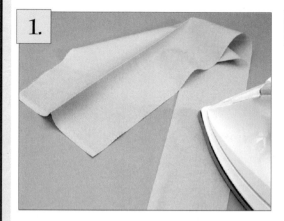

1. Cut the fabric at least twice the length of the finished ruffle. The width of the strip should be twice the width of the ruffles plus two seam allowances. Press this strip in half, wrong sides together.

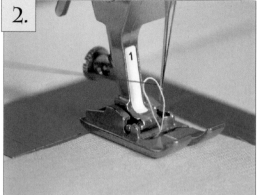

2. Starting 1″ from the edge, take one stitch. Pull the top thread tail, bringing the bobbin thread up though the fabric. Pull a length of bobbin thread as long as the piece to be gathered.

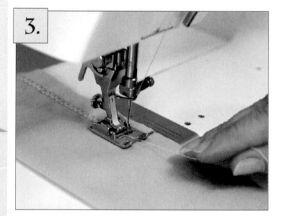

3. Set the machine for a wide zigzag and sew over the bobbin thread.

4. After stitching, pull the bobbin thread to gather the fabric.

CIRCULAR RUFFLES

This method of ruffle construction requires no gathering stitch. The ruffles are actually cut as circles creating a bias. They will stand up but have no additional bulk.

1. Draw a small circle. Measure from the edge of this circle the width of the finished ruffle. Draw a second circle around the small one. Add a seam allowance around the large circle and to the inside of the smaller one. There will now be four circles drawn.

2. Cut around outer circle, slice through to the smallest circle and cut around it. It will look like a sliced donut.

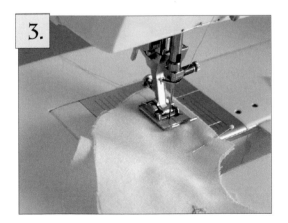

3. Sew several circles end to end until the ruffle is at the finished length. Finish the outside edge with a Serger Rolled Hem, page 75.

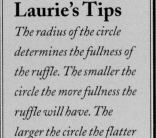

Laurie's Tips

The radius of the circle determines the fullness of the ruffle. The smaller the circle the more fullness the ruffle will have. The larger the circle the flatter the ruffle will lie.

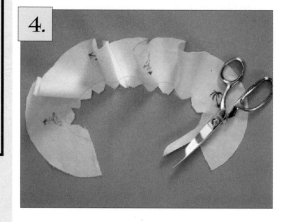

4. Clip the seam along the seam allowance and insert ruffle into the seam where desired.

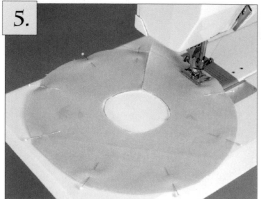

5. For lined ruffles, cut two fabric strips. With right sides together, sew the outside circle first. Trim, turn and press. Sew the rest of the circles together to form the length of ruffle needed.

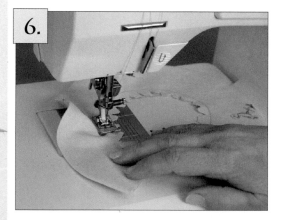

6. Sew the two layers of the inside circles together.

PIPING

Piping adds a sporty looking detail to cuffs, collars, or to the front of a shirt. It can add an outline of color to a simple, plain blouse.

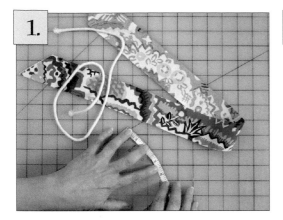

1. Cut a piece of cord the length of the seam plus 2". The width of the cord for blouses should be between $\frac{1}{16}$" to $\frac{1}{2}$".

2. Cut a strip of fabric the same length as the cord. The width of this strip should equal the circumference of the cord plus 1" for seam allowances.

Laurie's Tips

Piping is defined as a fabric-covered cord with seam allowances that can be inserted into a seam. If the fabric strip is cut on the bias, it will curve around collars, yokes or other curved seams more smoothly. Cutting the fabric on the bias also becomes a design decision. Stripes and plaids take on a different look when cut on the bias.

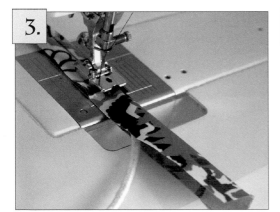

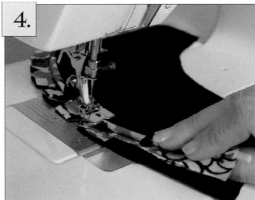

3. Wrap the fabric strip around the cord, right side out, and stitch as close to the cord as possible using a zipper or piping foot.

4. Sew the finished piping to the right side of one section of your collar or blouse front, using a contrasting thread in the bobbin. With right sides together, pin the layers. Stitch close to the piping using the bobbin thread as a guide.

HEMSTITCHING

Traditional hemstitching is created by pulling threads from the fabric by hand and stitching around the holes that are formed. Achieve the same effect by using a wing needle on your sewing machine.

Laurie's Tips

If hemstitching on collars or cuffs, construct the piece following the pattern directions but eliminating the interfacing. Press, using spray starch, until the piece is very crisp. Let the piece dry then begin hemstitching, using a foot that allows good visibility. After the decorative stitching is done, sew the collar or cuffs to the blouse. If the hemstitching is to be done on the front of the blouse, starch the pattern pieces and press until stiff. Hemstitch with the wing needle. Continue constructing the blouse without any interfacing in this area except under the buttonhole and buttons.

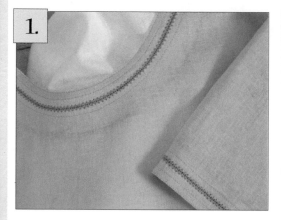

1.

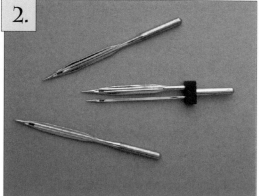

2.

1. Natural, woven fabrics are the best for this technique, because the needle pierces the fabric more easily and the holes stay open more readily.

2. A wing needle is a wide, flat needle that creates holes in the fabric. There are single and double wing needles with sizes #100 and #120 for the largest holes.

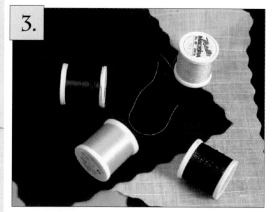

3.

4.

3. After you have chosen a woven fabric, thread is the next choice. Use a fine, #40 weight thread. Rayon or silk thread will add sheen or try a metallic thread for some glitter.

4. For hemstitching, select any stitch on your machine where the needle goes in the same hole more than once. Some good choices are the multi-zig zag, blind hem or daisy stitch.

METRIC EQUIVALENTS: INCHES TO MILLIMETRES (MM) AND CENTIMETRES (CM)

Inches	MM	CM	Inches	CM	Inches	CM
⅛	3	0.3	9	22.9	30	76.2
¼	6	0.6	10	25.4	31	78.7
⅜	10	1.0	11	27.9	32	81.3
½	13	1.3	12	30.5	33	83.8
⅝	16	1.6	13	33.0	34	86.4
¾	19	1.9	14	35.6	35	88.9
⅞	22	2.2	15	38.1	36	91.4
1	25	2.5	16	40.6	37	94.0
1¼	32	3.2	17	43.2	38	96.5
1½	38	3.8	18	45.7	39	99.1
1¾	44	4.4	19	48.3	40	101.6
2	51	5.1	20	50.8	41	104.1
2½	64	6.4	21	53.3	42	106.7
3	76	7.6	22	55.9	43	109.2
3½	89	8.9	23	58.4	44	111.8
4	102	10.2	24	61.0	45	114.3
4½	114	11.4	25	63.5	46	116.8
5	127	12.7	26	66.0	47	119.4
6	152	15.2	27	68.6	48	121.9
7	178	17.8	28	71.1	49	124.5
8	203	20.3	29	73.7	50	127.0

YARDS TO INCHES TO METRES

Yards	Inches	Metres	Yards	Inches	Metres
⅛	4.5	0.11	1⅛	40.5	1.03
¼	9	0.23	1¼	45	1.14
⅜	13.5	0.34	1⅜	49.5	1.26
½	18	0.46	1½	54	1.37
⅝	22.5	0.57	1⅝	58.5	1.49
¾	27	0.69	1¾	63	1.60
⅞	31.5	0.80	1⅞	67.5	1.71
1	36	0.91	2	72	1.83

INDEX